# The Anxiety Toolkit for Teens

A Simple And Hands-on Workbook With Powerful DBT And CBT Tools To Overcome Teen Stress And Anxiety And Improve Mental Health

*Bella Clark*

# Copyright © 2022 by Bella Clark

All rights reserved. No part of this publication may be reproduced, stored or transmitted in any form or by any means, electronic, mechanical, photocopying, recording, scanning, or otherwise without written permission from the publisher. It is illegal to copy this book, post it to a website, or distribute it by any other means without permission.

First edition

# A FREE GIFT TO OUR READERS!

**Printable Journal With Daily Prompts & Printable Anxiety Worksheets**

Get your free gift here:

# Table of Contents

Introduction ........................................................................................................... 1
How to Use ............................................................................................................ 3
The Anxiety Crew .................................................................................................. 5
Your Body's Response to "Threat" ...................................................................... 11
Book 1: Anxiety Free For Teens – Physical Techniques ..................................... 27
Book 2: Anxiety Free For Teens – Mental Habits ............................................... 47
Book 3: Anxiety Free For Teens – Master Your Feelings ................................... 67
Book 4: Anxiety Free For Teens – Behavioral Tools .......................................... 75
Help Others .......................................................................................................... 89
Quotes on Positive Thinking ................................................................................ 95
Positive Affirmations ........................................................................................... 97
Resources ............................................................................................................. 98

# Introduction

If you're reading this book, chances are you're a teenager juggling a lot of responsibilities and demands on a daily basis. Whether it's schoolwork, extracurricular activities, friendships, or family expectations, it's understandable to feel stressed and anxious at times. In fact, it's completely normal to experience anxiety as a teenager.

But if your anxiety is starting to interfere with your daily life and prevent you from doing the things you enjoy, it might be time to take some action. That's where this book comes in. Inside, you'll find the best tools and strategies to help you manage your anxiety and find a sense of calm in the midst of all the chaos. We'll explore different techniques for coping with anxiety, such as relaxation techniques, mindfulness, and self-care. You'll also learn how to talk to friends and family about your anxiety and seek out professional help if you need it.

So let's get started on your journey towards feeling more in control of your anxiety. Remember, you don't have to face it alone – there are people and resources available to support you.

Learning about anxiety is an important step towards finding ways to control it. When you understand what anxiety is and how it affects your body and mind, you can start to identify your own personal triggers and find ways to manage them. By learning about different techniques for coping with anxiety, you can find the ones that work best for you and build a toolkit of strategies to use when you start to feel anxious.

It's important to remember that everyone's experience with anxiety is different, and there is no one-size-fits-all solution. What works for one person might not work for another, so it's important to be open-minded and willing to try different approaches. It may take some trial and error to find what works best for you, but with patience and persistence, you can learn how to manage your anxiety and lead a happier, healthier life.

This book is divided into four main sections, each focusing on different tools and strategies for managing anxiety.

## HOW TO USE

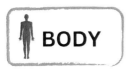

The first section, "Body," covers techniques for managing anxiety through physical means. This includes relaxation techniques such as deep breathing, progressive muscle relaxation, and meditation. These techniques can help to calm the body's natural fight or flight response and promote a sense of relaxation and calm.

The second section, "Mind," focuses on techniques for managing anxiety through cognitive means. This includes strategies such as mindfulness, positive thinking, and reframing negative thoughts. These techniques can help you to become more aware of your thoughts and feelings and find ways to change the way you think about anxiety-provoking situations.

The third section, "Emotions," covers techniques for managing anxiety through emotional means. This includes strategies such as self-care, expressing and processing emotions, and finding support from friends and family. These techniques can help you to better understand and cope with your emotions and find healthy ways to manage stress and anxiety.

The fourth and final section, "Behavior," focuses on techniques for managing anxiety through behavioral means. This includes strategies such as setting goals, breaking tasks down into smaller steps, and finding healthy ways to cope with stress. These techniques can help you to take control of your behavior and find more productive ways to manage your anxiety.

Throughout the book, you'll find real-life examples and exercises to help you apply these techniques in your own life and find the ones that work best for you. We'll delve into the science behind anxiety and explore the different types and symptoms. We'll also discuss the potential causes of anxiety and how it can be treated. By the end of this book, you'll have a better understanding of anxiety and feel equipped with the knowledge and skills to manage it in your daily life.

# The Anxiety Crew

## Meet Ronnie the Lion - Anxiety

Imagine that anxiety is a wild animal, like a lion, constantly prowling around in your mind. Let's call it Ronnie. It can be unpredictable and can strike at any moment, leaving you feeling on edge and vulnerable. Just like a lion, anxiety has the power to overpower you and take control of your thoughts and actions. It can make you feel like you are constantly running from something, even if there is no real threat present.

Anxiety is like a lion in the sense that it can be difficult to tame and control. It takes a lot of effort and work to try to keep it in check, and sometimes it can feel like an uphill battle. But just like how a lion can be trained and domesticated with patience and care, it is possible to learn how to manage and cope with anxiety. It may not always be easy, but with the right tools and support, you can learn how to coexist with this powerful animal and not let it rule your life.

There are many different activities that can cause anxiety for teenagers. Here are a few examples:

- ☑ **School:** School can be a major source of anxiety for teenagers. This can include things like studying for exams, giving presentations, or meeting new people.

- ☑ **Extracurricular activities:** Participating in extracurricular activities, such as sports, music, or clubs, can be a great way to make friends and have fun. However, they can also be stressful, especially if there is a lot of pressure to succeed.

- ☑ **Social situations:** Navigating social situations, such as making friends or dating, can be anxiety-provoking for teenagers.

- ☑ **Family expectations:** Meeting the expectations of parents or other family members can be stressful for teenagers.

- ☑ **Future plans:** Thinking about the future, such as choosing a college or career, can cause anxiety for teenagers.

- ☑ **Health:** Health concerns, such as feeling sick or worrying about physical appearance, can cause anxiety for teenagers.

- ☑ **Personal problems:** Personal problems, such as financial worries or relationship issues, can also cause anxiety for teenagers.

## Meet Annie the Anteater - Worry

Annie the Anteater represents worry. Just like an anteater, she has a long, slender snout that she uses to sniff out potential problems or threats. When people worry about something, Annie is constantly searching and scavenging, trying to find something to worry about. She can be demanding and persistent, always wanting your attention and energy.

When Annie is active, she can consume a lot of your mental and emotional resources, just like how an anteater can consume a large number of ants in one sitting. She can drain you and make you feel exhausted, and it can be hard to shake her off or get her out of your mind. Just like how an anteater can be hard to evade in the wild, worry can be hard to escape when it takes hold.

However, just like how an anteater can be managed and coexisted with in nature, worry can be managed and coped with. With the right tools and strategies, it is possible to learn how to manage Annie and not let her control your life.

## Meet Lucy the Zebra - Fear

Lucy the Zebra is a creature that represents fear. Just like a zebra, Lucy is constantly on the lookout for danger and threats. When you fear something, Lucy is always on high alert, ready to run at a moment's notice. She is fast and agile, able to quickly flee from danger.

When Lucy is active, she can make you feel jumpy and jittery, just like how a zebra might feel if it is being chased by a predator. She can also make you feel like you are constantly on edge, waiting for something bad to happen. Just like how a zebra might freeze or flee when faced with a threat, fear can cause you to react in similar ways.

# Meet Milo the Baboon - Stress

Milo the Baboon is a creature that represents stress. Milo is constantly wary of potential threats or challenges. When you are stressed, Milo is always ready to take action and find ways to cope with the stressors.

When Milo is active, he can make you feel overwhelmed and scattered, just like how a baboon might feel if it is being chased by a predator. He can also make you feel like you are constantly juggling a lot of tasks and responsibilities, trying to keep everything in balance. Just like how a baboon might use its physical strength and agility to deal with stress, you might find yourself relying on similar coping mechanisms to deal with stress.

# Meet Callie the Ostrich - Panic

Callie the Ostrich represents panic. When you are panicked, Callie is always ready to look for ways to cope with the panic.

When Callie is triggered, she can make you feel like you are in a state of emergency, just like how an ostrich might behave in a tricky situation that causes it to be in panic. She can also make you feel like you are out of control and unable to think clearly, just like how an ostrich might become panicked and disoriented when faced with a threat.

## Anxiety Crew

# Your Body's Response to "Threat"

The fight, flight or freeze response, also known as the fight or flight response, is a physiological reaction that occurs in response to a perceived threat. It is an evolutionary response that has developed in humans and other animals as a means of survival.

In animals, the fight, flight or freeze response is often triggered by the presence of a predator. When an animal perceives a threat, it has three main options: fight, flee, or freeze. If it has the ability to fight and defend itself, it may choose to do so in order to protect itself or its territory. If it does not have the ability to fight, it may choose to flee in order to escape the threat. If it is unable to fight or flee, it may choose to freeze in order to avoid being noticed by the predator.

Examples of animals using the fight, flight or freeze response include:

**Deer**
When a deer perceives a threat, it will often flee in order to escape. If it is unable to flee, it may try to hide or freeze in order to avoid being noticed. If it is cornered and has no other options, it may try to fight in order to defend itself.

**Rabbit**
When a rabbit perceives a threat, it will often freeze in order to avoid being noticed by the predator. If it is unable to freeze, it may try to escape by running or hiding. If it is cornered and has no other options, it may try to fight in order to defend itself.

**Squirrel**
When a squirrel perceives a threat, it will often try to escape by climbing a tree or running away. If it is unable to escape, it may try to defend itself by biting or scratching the predator. If it is cornered and has no other options, it may try to freeze in order to avoid being noticed.

**Anteater**
When an anteater perceives a threat, it will often try to escape by running away. If it is unable to escape, it may try to defend itself by using its sharp claws or strong jaws. If it is cornered and has no other options, it may try to freeze.

## What happens in our bodies during FFF?

During the fight, flight or freeze response, several physiological changes occur in the body in order to prepare for action. Here is a brief overview of what happens:

- ☑ The brain sends a signal to the adrenal gland to release adrenaline, which prepares the body for action.
- ☑ The heart rate increases, causing an increase in blood flow to the muscles.
- ☑ The muscles tense up, preparing the body for action.
- ☑ The blood vessels in the skin constrict, reducing blood flow to the skin and increasing blood flow to the muscles.
- ☑ The pupils dilate, allowing more light to enter the eyes and improving vision.
- ☑ The senses become heightened, allowing the individual to be more aware of their surroundings.
- ☑ The body becomes more alert and responsive, allowing the individual to react quickly to the perceived threat.

If the individual chooses to fight or flee, their muscles will be ready for action and they will be able to move quickly. If the individual chooses to freeze, they will become still and try to blend in with their surroundings in order to avoid being noticed.

Overall, the fight, flight or freeze response is an automatic response that is triggered in response to a perceived threat. It is a natural and necessary response that has evolved in humans and other animals as a means of survival.

There are many different situations that can trigger the fight, flight or freeze response in humans. Some common examples include:

### Social situations
Being in a social situation that feels uncomfortable or threatening, such as giving a public speech or meeting new people.

### Performance pressure
Feeling pressure to perform or succeed, such as during a job interview or a sporting event.

### Health concerns
Worries about health, such as the fear of becoming sick or being injured.

### Financial stress
Financial stress, such as worrying about paying bills or meeting financial obligations.

### Relationship issues
Relationship problems, such as conflicts with friends or family members.

Overall, the fight, flight or freeze response can be triggered by a wide range of situations that are perceived as threatening or stressful. It is a natural and necessary response that helps individuals to cope with these situations and find ways to protect themselves or escape from danger.

# Anxiety Disorders

The fight or flight response is a natural physiological response that takes place in response to a perceived threat. This response is hardwired into the human body and is meant to protect us from harm by either fighting the threat or fleeing from it. However, in modern times, the fight or flight response can be unnecessarily triggered by everyday stressors and can cause anxiety when it is not helpful for an individual.

One way that the fight or flight response can be unnecessarily triggered is through the perception of a threat. For example, if an individual perceives a work deadline as a threat to their well-being, they may experience the fight or flight response even though the perceived threat is not actually life-threatening. Similarly, if an individual perceives social situations as threatening, they may experience the fight or flight response even in non-threatening social situations.

Another way that the fight or flight response can be unnecessarily triggered is through negative thoughts and beliefs. If an individual has negative thoughts or beliefs about themselves or the world around them, they may be more likely to perceive everyday stressors as threats and experience the fight or flight response.

When the fight or flight response is unnecessarily triggered, it can cause anxiety in individuals. Anxiety is a natural response to stress and can be helpful in small doses, but when it is experienced excessively or in response to non-threatening situations, it can be debilitating. The physical symptoms of anxiety, such as rapid heartbeat, sweaty palms, and difficulty breathing, can be distressing and can interfere with an individual's ability to function in daily life.

There are different types of anxiety disorders, each with its unique set of triggers. Here are the most common anxiety disorders organized by their triggers:

### Specific phobias
These are intense fears of specific objects or situations, such as heights, snakes, or flying. The trigger for a specific phobia is the presence or anticipation of the feared object or situation.

### Social anxiety disorder
This is a fear of social situations or being judged by others. The trigger for social anxiety disorder is often social situations or the anticipation of having to interact with others.

### Panic disorder
This is characterized by sudden and intense episodes of fear, called panic attacks. The trigger for panic attacks can be diverse and may not always be apparent. Some common triggers include stress, caffeine, and exercise.

### Generalized anxiety disorder
This is characterized by excessive and persistent worry about a variety of topics. The trigger for generalized anxiety disorder is often chronic stress or a tendency to worry excessively.

### Obsessive-compulsive disorder
This is characterized by obsessive thoughts and compulsive behaviors. The trigger for obsessive-compulsive disorder is often the presence of obsessive thoughts or the inability to perform certain behaviors.

### Post-traumatic stress disorder
This is a type of anxiety disorder that can occur after a person has experienced or witnessed a traumatic event. The trigger for post-traumatic stress disorder is the presence or anticipation of a reminder of the traumatic event.

# PHOBIA

A phobia is an intense fear of a specific object or situation that is out of proportion to the actual danger posed by the object or situation. Phobias are a type of anxiety disorder and can cause significant distress and interfere with an individual's ability to function in daily life. Common phobias include a fear of heights, a fear of snakes, and a fear of flying.

**Example: A phobia of snakes**

Here are five negative thoughts that a person with a phobia of snakes might have in the presence of a snake:

It's important to note that these thoughts are irrational and not based in reality, but they can feel very real and intense to someone with a phobia of snakes.

If an individual has a phobia of snakes (also known as ophidiophobia), they may experience intense fear, anxiety, and panic in the presence of a snake or even the anticipation of encountering a snake. This fear can manifest in a variety of behaviors, including:

**Avoidance:** The individual may go to great lengths to avoid being near a snake, such as avoiding certain areas or situations where they might encounter a snake.

**Panic:** The individual may experience panic attacks in the presence of a snake or the anticipation of encountering a snake. Panic attacks are characterized by symptoms such as rapid heartbeat, shortness of breath, and feelings of terror or impending doom.

**Crying:** The individual may experience intense fear and become overwhelmed, leading to crying or tearfulness.

**Screaming:** The individual may react to the presence of a snake by screaming or making other loud noises.

**Freezing:** The individual may become paralyzed with fear and be unable to move or speak in the presence of a snake.

It's important to note that these behaviors are a natural response to the intense fear that is associated with a phobia, and they are not under the individual's conscious control.

Social anxiety is an anxiety disorder that is characterized by a fear of social situations or being judged by others. This fear can be so intense that it interferes with an individual's ability to participate in everyday activities, such as attending school or work, or making small talk with strangers. People with social anxiety may experience physical symptoms of anxiety, such as rapid heartbeat, sweaty palms, and difficulty speaking, in social situations. They may also have negative thoughts about themselves and their ability to interact with others. Social anxiety can be treated through therapy, medication, and self-help strategies such as relaxation techniques and exposure therapy.

Social anxiety can occur in a variety of social situations, including:

- ☑ **Parties or gathering**
- ☑ **Public speaking or presentations**
- ☑ **Meeting new people**
- ☑ **Making small talk with strangers**
- ☑ **Asking someone out on a date**
- ☑ **Attending social events or functions**
- ☑ **Participating in group activities**
- ☑ **Eating or drinking in front of others**
- ☑ **Going to the store or running errands**
- ☑ **Using public restrooms**

It's important to note that the severity of social anxiety can vary from person to person. Some people may only experience social anxiety in certain situations, while others may experience it in many different social situations. Social anxiety can also occur at different levels of intensity. Some people may only experience mild anxiety in social situations, while others may experience intense anxiety and panic.

Here are some examples of negative thoughts that a person may have when talking to strangers:

IIt's important to note that these thoughts are often irrational and not based in reality. However, they can feel very real and intense to someone experiencing social anxiety, and they can lead to significant distress and interfere with an individual's ability to interact with others.

If you experience social anxiety while talking to a stranger, you may exhibit a variety of behaviors, including:

**Avoiding eye contact:** You may avoid looking at the stranger or maintain brief eye contact to avoid being perceived as anxious or nervous.

**Fidgeting:** You may fidget with your hands, clothing, or other objects to distract yourself or try to release nervous energy.

**Mumbling or speaking quietly:** You may speak softly or mumble to avoid drawing attention to yourself or because you feel self-conscious about your voice.

**Avoiding conversation:** You may struggle to come up with things to say or may avoid speaking altogether to avoid making mistakes or feeling judged.

**Sweating:** You may experience sweaty palms or increased sweating due to physical symptoms of anxiety.

**Rapid heartbeat:** You may experience a rapid heartbeat due to the physical symptoms of anxiety.

It's important to note that these behaviors are a natural response to the anxiety and fear that is associated with social anxiety, and they are not under your conscious control.

# GENERALIZED ANXIETY DISORDER

Generalized anxiety disorder (GAD) is an anxiety disorder distinguished through persistent and excessive worry about a broad range of topics. People with GAD may worry about things such as their health, finances, relationships, or the well-being of loved ones, even when there is no apparent reason to worry. This excessive worry can interfere with an individual's ability to function in daily life and can lead to physical symptoms such as difficulty sleeping, fatigue, and muscle tension.

Here are some examples of situations in which GAD might occur for someone. A person with GAD may worry excessively about:

- ☑ **Work:** job performance, meeting deadlines, or job security.
- ☑ **School:** grades, test performance, or fitting in with their peers.
- ☑ **Relationships:** relationships or the well-being of loved ones.
- ☑ **Finances:** financial situation or the possibility of experiencing financial hardship.
- ☑ **Health:** health or the health of loved ones, even when there is no apparent reason to worry.
- ☑ **Decision-making:** making the right decisions, even when the decisions are minor or insignificant.

It's important to note that GAD can be triggered by many different situations and that the severity of GAD can vary from person to person. Some people may only experience GAD in certain situations, while others may experience it more consistently.

Here are some examples of negative thoughts that a person might have while experiencing generalized anxiety disorder (GAD):

People with GAD may have difficulty controlling their worry and may experience physical symptoms such as tension, muscle aches, and difficulty sleeping. GAD can also lead to negative behavior patterns, including:

**Procrastination:** Worrying about the outcome of a task or event can make it difficult for a person with GAD to start or complete the task, leading to procrastination.

**Avoidance:** A person with GAD may avoid certain situations, people, or activities that trigger their anxiety in order to reduce their distress.

**Dependency:** Some people with GAD may become overly dependent on others for support and reassurance, which can interfere with their ability to manage their anxiety and lead to an unhealthy dynamic in relationships.

**Impulsivity:** Anxiety can lead to impulsive behavior as a person tries to escape or reduce their anxiety.

**Difficulty making decisions:** Worrying about potential negative outcomes can make it difficult for a person with GAD to make decisions, even when it comes to simple tasks.

**Difficulty concentrating:** Anxiety can interfere with a person's ability to focus and concentrate, which can affect their performance at work or school.

# PANIC DISORDER

Panic disorder is a mental health disorder characterized by recurrent, unexpected panic attacks. A panic attack is a sudden, unexpected, and intense episode of fear or anxiety that can involve a range of physical and emotional symptoms, including rapid heartbeat, difficulty breathing, chest pain, dizziness, and feelings of impending doom. Panic attacks typically peak within a few minutes and may last for several hours.

People with panic disorder often worry excessively about having another panic attack and may avoid situations in which they have previously experienced a panic attack. This avoidance can significantly impact their daily lives and may lead to social isolation and difficulty functioning at work or school. Panic disorder is treatable with therapy and medication.

# POST-TRAUMATIC DISORDER

Post-traumatic stress disorder (PTSD) is a mental health disorder that can develop after an individual experiences or witnesses a traumatic event, such as a natural disaster, a car accident, a terrorist attack, or military combat. Symptoms of PTSD include re-experiencing the event that caused the trauma through nightmares or flashbacks, avoidance of reminders of the event, negative changes in mood and thinking, and changes in physical and emotional reactions. For example, an individual with PTSD may feel anxious, irritable, or have difficulty sleeping.

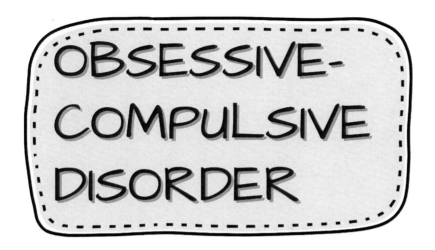

Obsessive-compulsive disorder (OCD) is a mental health disorder characterized by obsessions (recurrent, unwanted thoughts or ideas) and compulsions (mental acts or repetitive behaviors) that a person feels driven to perform in order to reduce anxiety or distress. Obsessions and compulsions can take many different forms and may vary from person to person.

Examples of obsessions include:

- ☑ **Fear of contamination or germs**
- ☑ **Unwanted violent thoughts**
- ☑ **Excessive concern about order or symmetry**
- ☑ **Persistent doubt about actions or decisions**

Examples of compulsions include:

- ☑ **Excessive hand washing or cleaning**
- ☑ **Checking things repeatedly (e.g., locks, appliances)**
- ☑ **Repeatedly arranging objects in a specific way**
- ☑ **Counting, touching, or repeating words or phrases**

# Anxiety Free: Physical Techniques

While the physical reactions induced by the fight, flight, or freeze response cannot be stopped, they can be controlled. In this chapter, we will explore ways in which you can control your stress response and manage the physical reactions it produces. Understanding how to control your stress response is an important part of maintaining physical and emotional well-being. Let's get started!

Here is what you can do to control the physical reactions you experience during the FFF response.

During times of anxiety, the body's stress response is activated, which can cause changes in breathing. Specifically, the body may take in more oxygen through rapid or shallow breathing. This is known as hyperventilation. Hyperventilation can lead to a number of physical symptoms, such as lightheadedness, dizziness, and tingling in the hands and feet.

Breathing exercises help regulate the breath and reduce anxiety by bringing more oxygen into the body and helping to calm the nervous system. There are various breathing exercises that can be helpful for reducing anxiety.

Breathing exercises can be practiced anywhere and at any time and can help to calm the mind and the body, making them a useful tool for managing anxiety.

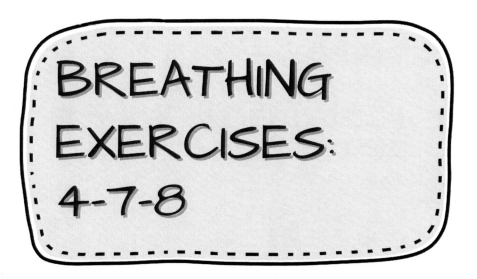
# BREATHING EXERCISES: 4-7-8

1. Position the tip of your tongue against the ridge of tissue right before your upper front teeth and keep it there throughout the exercise.

 2. Exhale fully through your mouth.

3. Close your mouth and inhale slowly through your nose while you count in your mind to four.

 4. Hold your breath and simultaneously count to seven in your mind.

5. Exhale fully through your mouth while you count to eight.

This completes one breath. Now inhale once more and repeat the cycle until you reach a total of four breaths.

**Recommended Frequency:** Min. 2x daily

**Helps with:** Anxiety

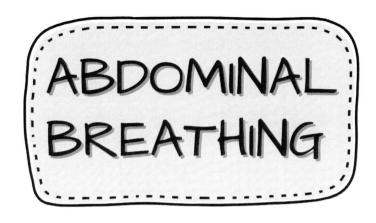

# ABDOMINAL BREATHING

Abdominal breathing, known as diaphragmatic breathing, is a breathing technique that involves focusing on the breath and using the diaphragm to inhale and exhale. This type of breathing can help to reduce anxiety by calming the nervous system and promoting relaxation. Here's how to practice abdominal breathing to reduce anxiety:

 Find a comfortable seated or lying down position.

 Position one hand on your abdomen and the other hand on your chest.

- Take a gradual, deep breath in through your nose, sensing your stomach expand as you inhale.

 Exhale slowly through your mouth, feeling your stomach contract.

Continue to focus on your breath and repeat this pattern for several minutes. It's generally recommended to practice abdominal breathing for at least 5-10 minutes at a time. It's also helpful to find a quiet, comfortable place to practice abdominal breathing so you can focus on your breath without distractions.

**Recommended Frequency:** Min. 2x daily

**Helps with:** Any type of anxiety

Mindful breathing is a form of meditation in which you focus your attention on your breath and use it as an anchor to the present moment. It involves paying attention to your breath as it goes in and out, without judgment or trying to change it in any way. The purpose of mindful breathing is to help you become more aware of your present experience and to cultivate a sense of calm and clarity. When you practice mindful breathing, you are training your mind to be more present and less caught up in thoughts, emotions, and stress. This can help to reduce anxiety, improve sleep, and increase overall well-being.

Here are some steps you can follow to practice mindful breathing as a way to reduce anxiety:

- ☑ Find a comfortable and silent place to sit or lie down. You can close your eyes if you'd like.

- ☑ Bring your attention to your breath. You can do this by feeling the sensation of the air entering and going out of your nostrils or the rise and fall of your chest or belly.

- ☑ As you continue to focus on your breath, you may notice that your mind wanders. This is normal! When you notice that your mind has wandered, slowly redirect your focus back to your breath.

- ☑ You can try to inhale while you count to four and exhale while you count to six. This can help to slow down your breath and relax your body. You can adjust the ratio of your inhale to exhale to find what works best for you.

- ☑ Continue to focus on your breath for several minutes. You can start with just a few minutes and gradually increase the amount of time you spend on mindful breathing.

| **Recommended Frequency:** | Any time you are anxious or stressed | **Helps with:** | Anxiety, Stress |
|---|---|---|---|

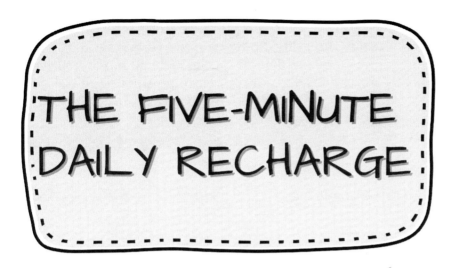

# THE FIVE-MINUTE DAILY RECHARGE

Cognitive behavioral therapy (CBT) is a form of therapy that focuses on how our thoughts, beliefs, and behaviors affect our feelings and actions. One common practice in CBT is the five-minute daily recharge. This is a simple but effective way to take a break, recharge your batteries, and refocus your thoughts.

Here are the steps for the five-minute daily recharge practice:

- ☑ Find a quiet, comfortable place to sit or lie down. You can do this practice anywhere, but it's best to find a place where you won't be interrupted or distracted.

- ☑ Set a timer for five minutes. It's important to stick to the time limit so that you don't get too relaxed and fall asleep.

- ☑ Close your eyes and take several deep breaths. Focus on the sensation of the air entering and leaving your body.

- ☑ Bring to mind a image or place that makes you feel calm and relaxed. This could be a beach, a mountain scene, a favorite vacation spot, or anything else that brings you peacc and joy.

- ☑ Imagine yourself in this place, using your senses to fully experience it. What do you see? What do you hear? What do you smell? What do you feel?

- ☑ When the timer goes off, gradually open your eyes and take a moment to return to the present. If you feel rested and recharged, great! If not, you can repeat the practice as needed.

| **Recommended Frequency:** | Any time you are anxious or stressed | **Helps with:** | Anxiety, Stress |
|---|---|---|---|

You can do the five-minute daily recharge practice any time you need to take a break and refocus your thoughts. Some people find it helpful to do it first thing in the morning to start the day off on the right foot, while others prefer to do it in the afternoon to help them get through the rest of the day. It's completely up to you and what works best for your schedule and needs.

# GROUNDING EXERCISES

Grounding exercises are a type of coping technique that can be used to manage anxiety and reduce stress. They are designed to help you stay present in the moment and bring your attention back to your senses, rather than getting caught up in racing thoughts or worrying about the future. Grounding exercises can be a helpful tool to have in your anxiety-management toolkit, as they can help you feel more in control and more centered when you're feeling overwhelmed.

There are many different types of grounding exercises, but they all have one thing in common: they involve focusing on something in the present moment to help you feel more connected to the here and now. Some common grounding exercises include:

 5-4-3-2-1

 **Deep breathing**

 **Body scan**

 **Progressive muscle relaxation**

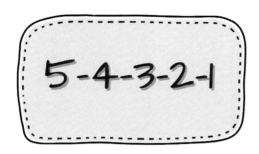

This involves looking around and identifying five things you can see, four things you can immediately touch, three things you are able to hear, two things you are able to smell, and one thing you can taste. This can help you bring your attention back to your senses and the present moment.

Example: Flower

> ☑ Close your eyes and take five deep breaths, focusing on the feeling of the air entering and going out of your body.
>
> ☑ Open your eyes and look at the flower. Notice four specific details about the flower, such as the color of the petals, the shape of the stem, the texture of the leaves, and the pattern on the center of the flower.
>
> ☑ Hold the flower in your hand and examine it more closely. Notice three more details, such as the faint fragrance of the flower, the way the petals feel against your skin, and the movement of the flower as you turn it in your hand.
>
> ☑ Bring the flower to your nose and take a deep inhale, noticing the scent of the flower and how it changes as you exhale. Notice two more details, such as the subtle shifts in the color of the petals as you move them in the light, and the way the flower feels in your hand as you adjust your grip.
>
> ☑ Hold the flower in front of you and spend a minute simply observing it and letting your thoughts and feelings come and go without judgment. Notice one thing you appreciate about the flower, such as the way it brightens up a room or the way it reminds you of a special memory.

# DEEP BREATHING

Taking slow, deep breaths will help you relax and calm your nervous system. You can focus on the sensation of the air entering and leaving your body, or count each breath as you inhale and exhale.

# BODY SCAN

This involves lying down or sitting comfortably and focusing on each part of your body, starting at your toes and working your way up to the top of your head. As you focus on each part, take several deep breaths and try to relax any tension you may be holding.

# PROGRESSIVE MUSCLE RELAXATION

This involves tensing and relaxing each muscle group in your body, starting with your toes and working your way up to the top of your head. As you tense each muscle, hold for a few seconds, then release and notice the difference in how the muscle feels.

Grounding exercises can be done anytime and anywhere, and you can choose the one that works best for you in the moment. They can be especially helpful when you're feeling anxious or overwhelmed, as they can help you refocus your thoughts and bring some calm to the present moment.

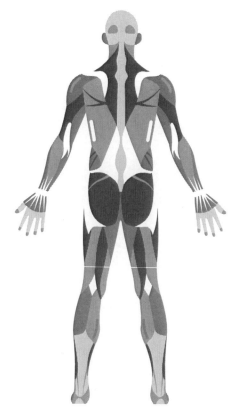

**Dialectical Behavior Therapy (DBT)** is a form of cognitive-behavioral therapy that was developed by Marsha M. Linehan to help individuals who struggle with emotion regulation, particularly those who have a history of self-harm or suicidal thoughts. DBT focuses on helping individuals develop skills in four main areas: mindfulness, emotion regulation, distress tolerance, and interpersonal effectiveness.

The safety and reconstruction skills taught in DBT are designed to help individuals cope with overwhelming emotions and crisis situations. These skills are typically taught in a group therapy setting and may be practiced during individual therapy sessions as well.

Here is a step-by-step guide to the safety and reconstruction skills taught in DBT:

**Identify and prioritize your values:** This involves identifying what is most important to you in life and making a plan to align your actions with these values.

**Develop a crisis survival plan:** This involves creating a plan to follow when you are in a crisis or feeling overwhelmed. This plan should include strategies for managing your emotions, such as using deep breathing or progressive muscle relaxation techniques, as well as ways to reach out for support from friends, family, or a therapist.

**Learn to cope with intense emotions:** This involves learning strategies for managing strong emotions in a healthy way, such as using mindfulness techniques to stay present in the moment or using the acronym "IMPROVE" to identify and challenge negative thought patterns.

**Practice self-soothing:** This involves finding ways to comfort and calm yourself during times of distress, such as taking a warm bath or listening to calming music.

**Build a support network:** This involves identifying people in your life who you can turn to for support and encouragement, such as friends, family, or a therapist.

**Repair relationships:** This involves working to repair damaged relationships or conflicts with others, whether through forgiveness, apology, or simply finding ways to communicate more effectively.

**Practice self-care:** This involves taking care of your physical and emotional well-being, such as getting enough sleep, engaging in activities that bring you joy, and eating well.

**Find meaning and purpose:** This involves identifying your strengths and values and finding ways to use them to contribute to the world around you.

Here is an example of how the 5-4-3-2-1 exercise can be used as a safety and reconstruction skill in Dialectical Behavior Therapy (DBT):

- ☑ Close your eyes and take five deep breaths, focusing on the feeling of the air entering and leaving your body. This helps you ground yourself in the present moment and regulate your breathing.

- ☑ Open your eyes and look around the room. Notice four specific details about your surroundings, such as the color of the walls, the texture of the furniture, the patterns in the curtains, and the sounds you hear. This helps you engage your senses and shift your attention away from any negative thoughts or emotions.

- ☑ Hold a comforting object, such as a stuffed animal or a piece of jewelry, and examine it closely. Notice three more details about the object, such as the way it feels in your hand, the texture of the surface, and any patterns or designs. This helps you engage your senses and find comfort in a physical object.

- ☑ Take a moment to practice a self-soothing activity, such as listening to calming music or reciting a mantra to yourself. Notice two more details about the activity, such as the way the music makes you feel or the words of the mantra as you repeat them. This helps you find comfort and relaxation in the present moment.

- ☑ Spend a minute simply observing your thoughts and feelings as they come and go without judgment. Notice one thing you appreciate about yourself or your current situation, such as a strength or value that you have or something that brings you joy. This helps you find gratitude and perspective in the midst of difficult emotions.

# MIMICKING SAFETY

Mimicking safety is a technique that can be used to help regulate emotions and cope with anxiety in the moment. It involves physically mimicking the posture, facial expression, and vocal tone of someone who is calm and composed, even if you do not feel that way internally.

Here is a step-by-step guide to using mimicking safety in an anxious moment:

- ☑ Identify someone who seems calm and composed: This could be a friend, family member, or even a fictional character on TV or in a movie.

- ☑ Notice their posture: How are they standing or sitting? Are they upright and relaxed, or tense and hunched over?

- ☑ Mimic their posture: Stand or sit in a similar way, taking care to keep your body relaxed and upright.

- ☑ Notice their facial expression: Are they smiling or frowning? Do they have a relaxed or tense forehead and jaw?

- ☑ Mimic their facial expression: Try to adopt a similar facial expression, taking care to relax your forehead and jaw.

- ☑ Notice their vocal tone: Are they speaking in a low, calm voice, or a high, anxious one?

- ☑ Mimic their vocal tone: Try to speak in a similar way, taking care to keep your voice low and calm.

- ☑ Take several deep breaths: Focus on the sensation of the air entering and leaving your body, and try to let go of any negative thoughts or emotions.

By physically mimicking the posture, facial expression, and vocal tone of someone who is calm and composed, you can help regulate your own emotions and cope with anxiety in the moment.

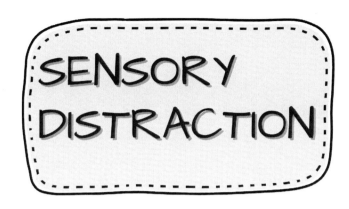

Sensory distraction involves using your senses to focus on something other than the source of your anxiety. This can be an effective way to calm yourself down in an anxious moment.

Here are some ways you can use sensory distraction:

- ☑ Sight: Look around you and find something interesting to focus on, such as a plant or a piece of art. Take in the details of the object and allow your mind to wander.

- ☑ Sound: Listen to calming music or white noise, such as the sound of rain or waves crashing. You can also try humming or singing to yourself.

- ☑ Touch: Engage in a tactile activity, such as squeezing a stress ball or knitting.

- ☑ Smell: Use essential oils or scented candles to create a calming aroma. You can also try sniffing a lemon or coffee beans, as these have been shown to have a calming effect.

- ☑ Taste: Suck on a piece of hard candy or chew gum to engage your sense of taste.

Remember to take slow, deep breaths as you engage in these activities. This can help to relax your body and reduce anxiety.

# BODY SCAN

A body scan is a mindfulness technique that involves paying attention to and relaxing each part of your body, starting from your toes and moving up to the top of your head. It can be a helpful way to calm yourself down during an anxious moment.

Here's how to do a body scan:

- ✓ Find a comfortable and silent place to lie down or sit.
- ✓ Close your eyes and take several deep breaths, focusing on the feeling of the breath moving in and out of your body.
- ✓ Slowly begin to bring your attention to each part of your body, starting with the toes and working your way up until you reach the top of your head. As you focus on each part of your body, take a deep breath and exhale, allowing yourself to relax and release any tension.
- ✓ When you reach the top of your head, take several more deep breaths and allow yourself to sink into a state of relaxation.

Remember to keep your focus on the present moment and try not to get caught up in any thoughts or worries. If your mind wanders, gently redirect your attention back to your body. You can do a body scan for as long as you like, but even a few minutes can be effective in helping to reduce anxiety.

# SQUEEZE HUG

A squeeze hug is a technique that involves using your own hands to give yourself a hug. It can be a helpful way to ground yourself and provide a sense of comfort during an anxious moment.

Here's how to do a squeeze hug:

- ✓ Place one hand on your chest and the other hand on your opposite shoulder.
- ✓ Gently squeeze your hands together, as if you are giving yourself a hug.
- ✓ Take several deep breaths and focus on the sensation of your hands on your body.
- ✓ Continue to hug yourself for as long as you need, allowing yourself to feel comforted and reassured.

You can also try variations of the squeeze hug by placing your hands on different parts of your body, such as your upper arms or your stomach. The key is to find a position that feels comforting and reassuring to you.

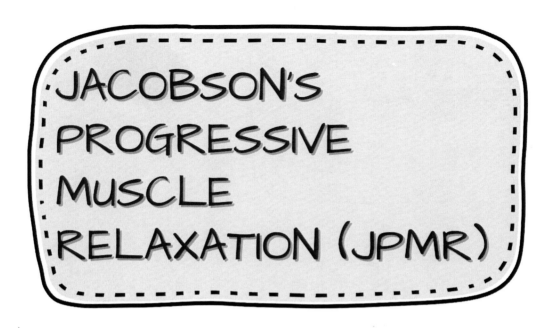

Jacobson's Progressive Muscle Relaxation (JPMR) is a technique that requires tensing and relaxing different muscle groups in the body in order to reduce tension and anxiety.

Here is a step-by-step guide on how to use JPMR in an anxious moment:

- ☑ Find a comfortable and silent place to sit or lie down.
- ☑ Close your eyes and take several deep breaths, focusing on the feeling of the breath moving in and out of your body.
- ☑ Begin by tensing the muscles in your toes and feet. Keep the tension for a few seconds, then slowly release and relax the muscles.
- ☑ Next, move up to your calves and tense the muscles in this area. Hold the tension for several seconds, then slowly release and relax the muscles.
- ☑ Continue working your way up through your body, relaxing and tensing each muscle group in turn: thighs, buttocks, stomach, back, arms, hands, neck, and face.
- ☑ When you have finished tensing and relaxing all the muscle groups, take a few more deep breaths and let yourself sink into a state of relaxation.

Remember to take your time and focus on the sensation of each muscle group as you tense and relax it. You may find it helpful to do the exercise with a recorded guided meditation or with a therapist.

## DIET

Diet can play a role in anxiety in several ways. Some research suggests that certain nutrients, such as omega-3 fatty acids and B vitamins, may be important for maintaining mental health and reducing anxiety. On the other hand, a diet high in processed foods, added sugars, and unhealthy fats may contribute to anxiety and other mental health problems.

One way to improve your diet and potentially reduce anxiety is to focus on eating a balanced diet that includes a broad range of whole, unprocessed foods. This can include:

- ☑ Fruits and vegetables: Try to have at least 5 servings per day.
- ☑ Lean proteins: Choose sources like poultry, fish, beans, and tofu.
- ☑ Whole grains: Look for options like whole wheat, quinoa, and oats.
- ☑ Healthy fats: Include sources like nuts, seeds, avocado, and olive oil.
- ☑ It may also be helpful to limit or avoid certain foods and beverages that may worsen anxiety, such as:
- ☑ Caffeine: This can be found in coffee, tea, soda, and some medications.
- ☑ Alcohol: While moderate alcohol consumption may be okay for some people, excessive drinking can increase anxiety.
- ☑ Highly processed foods: These can be high in added sugars, unhealthy fats, and preservatives, which may contribute to anxiety.

Remember that everyone is different, and what is effective for one individual may not be for another. It may be useful to speak with a registered dietitian or a healthcare provider if you have concerns about your diet and anxiety.

# SLEEP AND EXERCISE

Lack of sleep and exercise can contribute to anxiety in several ways. When you don't sleep enough, it can lead to physical and mental fatigue, which can increase your risk of anxiety and other mental health problems. Physical activity, on the other hand, has been shown to have several benefits for mental health, including reducing anxiety.

Here's how sleep and exercise can help reduce anxiety:

**Sleep:** Getting enough sleep is important for maintaining physical and mental health. When you sleep, your body has an opportunity to repair and restore itself. This can help to significantly reduce stress and improve overall well-being.

**Exercise:** Regular physical activity has been shown to reduce anxiety and improve mood. Exercise releases endorphins, which are chemicals in our brain that serve as natural painkillers and mood elevators. Exercise can also help to improve sleep and reduce stress, which can further help to reduce anxiety.

To improve your sleep and exercise habits, consider the following tips:

**Set a regular sleep schedule:** Plan to go to bed and wake up at the exact same time each day.

**Create a relaxing bedtime routine:** This can include activities like reading, taking a warm bath, or listening to soothing music.

**Get regular exercise:** Try to do at least 150 minutes of moderate-intensity workout per week, or 75 minutes of vigorous-intensity exercise.

**Avoid screens before you go to sleep:** The blue light emitted by your device screen can easily disrupt your natural sleep-wake cycle.

# Anxiety Free - Mental Habits

Irrational thoughts are negative or distorted thoughts that can contribute to anxiety and other mental health problems. Here are ten types of irrational thoughts, along with short examples of each:

**All-or-nothing thinking:** Seeing things as either completely good or completely bad, with no shades of gray. Example: "I either have to get an A on this test or I'm a complete failure."

**Overgeneralization:** Drawing broad conclusions based on a single event. Example: "I made one mistake at work, so I must be a complete failure at my job."

**Mental filter:** Focusing on the negative and ignoring the positive. Example: "I received several compliments about my presentation, but all I can think about is the one thing I messed up."

**Disqualifying the positive:** Dismissing positive experiences or accomplishments as not being important or meaningful. Example: "I received a promotion at work, but it was probably just a fluke."

**Jumping to conclusions:** Making assumptions without sufficient evidence. Example: "I haven't heard from my friend in a few days, so they must be mad at me."

**Magnification:** Blowing things out of proportion. Example: "I made one small mistake, so now everyone must think I'm completely incompetent."

**Minimization:** Downplaying your own accomplishments or the positive aspects of a situation. Example: "I worked really hard on that project, but it's not a big deal."

**Emotional reasoning:** Believing that your feelings reflect reality. Example: "I feel like a complete failure, so I must be a complete failure."

**"Should" statements:** Pressuring yourself to meet unrealistic standards. Example: "I should be able to handle everything perfectly, and anything less is a failure."

**Personalization:** Blaming yourself for things that are not your fault. Example: "The meeting didn't go well, so it must be because I'm not good enough."

It's important to remember that everyone has irrational thoughts from time to time. The key is to recognize when you're having them and to challenge them with more realistic and balanced thinking.

**Thought challenging** is a technique that involves questioning and examining your negative or irrational thoughts in order to replace them with more realistic and balanced ones. This can be helpful in combating anxiety and other mental health problems.

Here's an example of how to use thought challenging to combat irrational thoughts:

Let's say you have the irrational thought, "I'm going to make a fool of myself at the presentation."

- ☑ Step 1: Identify the thought. The first step is to recognize the irrational thought and acknowledge that it's just a thought, not a fact.

- ☑ Step 2: Examine the evidence. Next, look at the evidence for and against the thought. In this case, you might ask yourself: What is the evidence that I will make a fool of myself at the presentation? Have I made a fool of myself in the past? Are there times when I've done well in similar situations?

- ☑ Step 3: Identify the distortions. Look for any cognitive distortions, or irrational thinking patterns, in the thought. In this case, the thought might involve all-or-nothing thinking (seeing things as either completely good or completely bad) and magnification (blowing things out of proportion).

- ☑ Step 4: Generate alternative thoughts. Come up with more realistic and balanced alternative thoughts. For example: "I may make a mistake during the presentation, but that doesn't mean I'll make a fool of myself. I've done well in similar situations in the past, and I can handle any mistakes that come up."

Step 5: Test the alternative thoughts. Consider the evidence for and against the alternative thoughts. In this case, the evidence supports the idea that you may make a mistake during the presentation, but that doesn't mean you'll make a fool of yourself.

It may be helpful to write down your thoughts and work through the thought challenging process on paper. You can also work with a therapist to practice thought challenging and develop more realistic and balanced thinking patterns.

# THOUGHT RECORD

A thought record, also known as a cognitive diary, is a tool that can be used to identify and challenge irrational or negative thoughts. It involves writing down the specific trigger that led to a negative emotion or behavior, your initial reaction (emotion and behavior), the irrational thoughts that arose in response to the trigger, any evidence that the thought might be true, evidence that the thought might be false or exaggerated, a more balanced perspective on the situation, and any learning or insights gained from the experience.

Here is an example of how to use a thought record with the given headings:

**The trigger:**
Something happened that upset you, such as a criticism from a colleague or a disagreement with a friend.

**Reaction (emotion and behavior):**
You feel angry and lash out at the other person or withdraw from the situation.

**Irrational thoughts:**
You believe that the other person is intentionally trying to hurt you or that you are a failure because of what happened.

**Justification (Evidence that the thought is true):**
You point to past experiences where you were treated unfairly or where you made mistakes as evidence that your thought is true.

**Contradiction (Evidence that the thought is false):**
You consider alternative perspectives, such as the possibility that the other person was not trying to hurt you or that you have made many successes in the past despite any mistakes.

**Balanced thought:**
You recognize that the other person may have their own motivations and that mistakes are a natural part of life, but that does not make you a failure overall.

**Learning:**
You reflect on what you can learn from the experience and how you can handle similar situations in the future in a more balanced and healthy way.

By using a thought record in this way, you can learn to identify and challenge negative or irrational thoughts and gain a more balanced perspective on difficult situations.

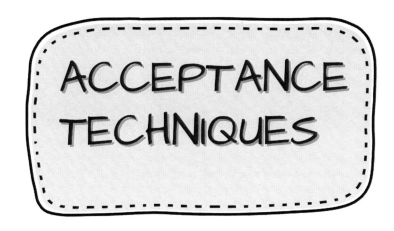

Acceptance techniques involve actively accepting and acknowledging negative thoughts, emotions, and physical sensations, rather than trying to fight or suppress them. These techniques can be helpful in dealing with anxiety because they allow you to experience anxiety in a more mindful and self-compassionate way, rather than getting caught up in a cycle of avoidance or distress.

The circle of control is a tool that can be used to manage stress by helping you focus on the things that you have control over and let go of the things that you cannot control.

Here is a step-by-step guide on how to use the circle of control to manage stress:

Identify the stress sources in your life. Make a list of the things that are causing you stress, including external factors (such as work or family responsibilities) and internal factors (such as negative thoughts or unhealthy habits).

Sort the items on your list into two categories: things that you have control over and things that you do not have control over.

For the things that you have control over, brainstorm specific actions you can take to address or reduce the stress.

Example: Things you have control over

> If work is a source of stress, you might try delegating tasks, setting boundaries, or finding ways to be more efficient.

Example: Things you don't have control over

> For the things that you do not have control over, practice acceptance and let go of the need to change them. This may involve finding ways to reframe your perspective on the situation, seeking support from others, or practicing mindfulness to help you stay present and grounded in the face of stress.

Take action on the things that you have identified as being within your control. This might involve making a plan and setting goals, or it might involve taking small steps each day to work towards your goals.

Practice self-care and manage your overall stress level by prioritizing activities that nourish your physical, emotional, and mental well-being. This might include getting enough sleep, eating a healthy diet, exercising regularly, or finding ways to relax and unwind.

By focusing on the things that you have control over and practicing self-care, you can effectively manage stress and improve your overall well-being.

# WORRY TREE

A worry tree is a tool that can be used to manage stress by helping you identify, analyze, and respond to your worries in a structured and proactive way.

Here is a step-by-step guide on how to use a worry tree to manage stress:

- ✓ Identify a specific worry that is causing you stress. This might be a concern about a specific event, such as an upcoming test or presentation, or a more general worry, such as a fear of failure or rejection.

- ✓ Write down the worry at the top of a piece of paper and draw a line from the worry to create the "trunk" of the tree.

- ✓ For each worry, brainstorm specific concerns or questions that stem from the worry. These might include things like "What if I don't do well on the test?" or "What if I'm rejected by my peers?". Write these concerns or questions as branches coming off the trunk of the tree.

- ✓ For each concern or question, identify any evidence or specific data that you have to support or refute the worry. Write this evidence or data as leaves on the branches of the tree.

- ✓ Review the worry tree and consider the evidence or data that you have collected. Is there more evidence to support or refute the worry? How likely is it that the worry will actually come true?

- ✓ Based on your review of the evidence, identify any specific actions you can take to address the worry or to prepare for a potential outcome. This might involve making a plan, seeking support from others, or finding ways to cope with the uncertainty.

By using a worry tree to structure and analyze your worries, you can gain a more balanced perspective and take proactive steps to manage stress.

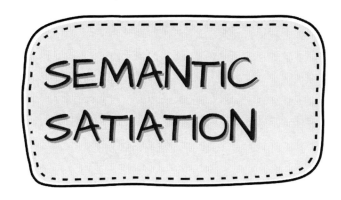

# SEMANTIC SATIATION

Semantic satiation is a phenomenon that occurs when a word or phrase is repeated so many times that it loses its meaning or impact. This can be a helpful tool for managing stress because it can interrupt automatic negative thoughts and help you become more aware of your thought patterns.

Here is a step-by-step guide on how to use semantic satiation to manage stress:

- ✓ Identify a specific negative thought or worry that is causing you stress. This might be a thought like "I'm not good enough" or "I'll never be able to do this."

- ✓ Write down the thought on a piece of paper or in a journal.

- ✓ Repeat the thought to yourself out loud, over and over again, for a period of time. You can also write the thought down repeatedly or say it to yourself silently in your head.

- ✓ Notice how the thought feels as you repeat it. Does it feel as impactful or meaningful as it did at first? Does it begin to feel silly or meaningless?

- ✓ Once you feel like the thought has lost its meaning or impact, take a break and do something else for a few minutes.

- ✓ Return to the thought after a break and notice if it feels any different. Does it still have the same power to stress you out?

- ✓ By repeating a negative thought until it loses its meaning or impact, you can interrupt automatic negative thinking and gain a more balanced perspective on the situation.

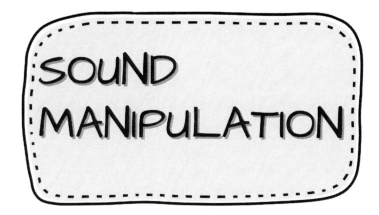 

# SOUND MANIPULATION

Sound manipulation is the use of specific sounds or music to alter your emotional state or cognitive functioning. This can be a helpful tool for managing stress because it can help you relax, focus, or shift your mindset.

Here are a few ways you can use sound manipulation to manage stress:

☑ Listen to calming music or nature sounds: Music and sounds that are slow, soothing, and lack lyrics or complex melodies can be helpful in reducing stress and anxiety. You can try listening to instrumental music, nature sounds, or guided relaxation tracks.

☑ Use white noise or ambient noise: White noise or ambient noise, such as the sound of rain or a fan, can help to mask distractions and create a sense of calm. You can use a white noise machine or app, or simply play a sound file on your phone or computer.

☑ Experiment with binaural beats: Binaural beats are specific sounds that can be used to alter brain wave activity and create specific states of consciousness. Some people find that listening to binaural beats can make them relax or focus, although the effectiveness of this technique is still being studied.

☑ Use music or sound to shift your mindset: Certain types of music or sounds can help to change your emotional state or shift your mindset. For example, upbeat or energizing music can help you feel more motivated or focused, while music with a slower tempo or more minor key can help you feel more relaxed or introspective.

# TRANSLATION

Here are the steps for using translation as a technique to help reduce anxiety:

- ☑ Identify a negative thought or belief that is contributing to your anxiety. This could be a thought like "I'm not good enough," "I can't handle this," or "I'm going to fail."

- ☑ Choose a foreign language that you are familiar with or are interested in learning. This could be a language that you already know or have studied in the past, or it could be a new language that you want to learn.

- ☑ Translate the negative thought or belief into the foreign language. You can use a dictionary or online translation tool to help with this step.

- ☑ Repeat the translated thought or belief to yourself several times, paying attention to the way it sounds and feels. Notice any changes in your emotional state or the impact of the thought on your anxiety.

- ☑ Continue to practice translating and repeating the thought or belief in the foreign language whenever you notice negative thoughts or beliefs that contribute to your anxiety. Over time, this can help to reduce the power of these thoughts and decrease your overall anxiety.

"I can't handle this." → "Wǒ shòu bùliǎo." (Mandarin Chinese)

Cognitive reappraisal is a technique used in cognitive-behavioral therapy (CBT) that involves changing the way you think about a situation in order to change your emotional response. This technique can be helpful for managing anxiety because the way we think about a situation can affect how anxious we feel. By changing our thoughts, we can change our emotional response to the situation.

Here are the steps for using cognitive reappraisal to reduce anxiety:

- ☑ Identify a situation that is causing you anxiety. This could be a specific event, a task you need to complete, or a social situation.

- ☑ Notice your thoughts and beliefs about the situation. What are you telling yourself about the situation? How are these thoughts contributing to your anxiety?

- ☑ Challenge these negative thoughts by asking yourself if they are really true. Are there any facts or evidence to support these thoughts? Are there any alternative perspectives that you could consider?

- ☑ Reframe the negative thought into a more balanced and positive perspective. For example, instead of thinking "I'm going to fail this test," try thinking "I may not get every answer right, but I have studied and am prepared. I'll do my best and that's all I can do."

Practice this reframing regularly, especially when you are feeling anxious. Over time, this can help to change your thought patterns and reduce anxiety.

Radical acceptance is a technique used in mindfulness-based therapies that involves accepting things as they are, rather than trying to change or resist them. This can be helpful for reducing anxiety because it allows us to let go of trying to control things that are outside of our control, which can be a major source of anxiety.

Here are the steps for using radical acceptance to reduce anxiety:

- ☑ Identify a situation that is causing you anxiety. This could be a specific event, a task you need to complete, or a social situation.

- ☑ Notice your thoughts and beliefs about the situation. What are you telling yourself about the situation? How are these thoughts contributing to your anxiety?

- ☑ Practice mindfulness by focusing on the present moment and accepting things as they are, rather than trying to change or resist them. This may involve accepting your own feelings and emotions, as well as the reality of the situation.

- ☑ Try to let go of the need to control the situation or the outcome. Remember that there are many things in life that are outside of our control, and that's okay.

- ☑ Practice radical acceptance regularly, especially when you are feeling anxious. Over time, this can help you to feel more at peace with the present moment and reduce anxiety.

It's important to keep in mind that practicing radical acceptance does not mean that you have to like a situation or that you can't take action to try to change it. It simply means that you are accepting things as they are in the present moment.

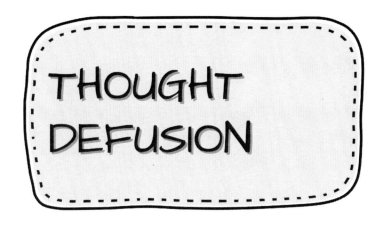

Thought defusion is a technique used in acceptance and commitment therapy (ACT) that involves stepping back from our thoughts and observing them without getting caught up in them. This can be helpful for reducing anxiety because it helps us to recognize that our thoughts are just thoughts, and not necessarily facts or reality.

Here are the steps for using thought defusion to reduce anxiety:

- ☑ Identify a negative thought or belief that is contributing to your anxiety. This could be a thought like "I'm not good enough," "I can't handle this," or "I'm going to fail."

- ☑ Notice how the thought makes you feel, and the physical sensations that go along with it.

- ☑ Try to step back from the thought and observe it as if it were a separate entity, rather than getting caught up in it. Imagine that the thought is a cloud moving through the sky, or a tree leaf floating down a stream.

- ☑ Repeat the thought to yourself in a detached, matter-of-fact way, without getting caught up in the emotional content. For example, instead of thinking "I'm not good enough," try saying to yourself "I'm having the thought that I'm not good enough."

- ☑ Practice thought defusion regularly, especially when you are feeling anxious. Over time, this can help you to recognize that your thoughts are just thoughts, and not necessarily facts or reality, which can reduce anxiety.

# MEDITATION

Here is an example of a situation in which a person who is anxious might benefit from meditation:

Sara is a college student who is struggling with anxiety. She has a lot of stress from schoolwork, and she often finds herself worrying about her grades and her future. She has trouble sleeping because she can't stop thinking about everything she has to do.

One day, Sara's friend suggests that she try meditation to help manage her anxiety. Sara is skeptical, but decides to give it a try. She downloads a meditation app and sets aside some time each day to practice.

At first, Sara finds it difficult to quiet her mind and stay focused on her breath. But with practice, she begins to feel more calm and centered. She notices that she is better able to handle the stress of school, and she is sleeping better at night. She also finds that she is less reactive to small setbacks and is more able to handle challenges as they come.

Here is how Sara can meditate:

- Find a silent, comfortable place to sit or lie down. You can take a seat with your feet on the ground, or you can sit cross-legged on a cushion or blanket. You can also lie down if that is more comfortable.

- Close your eyes and take several deep breaths. Inhale deeply and slowly through your nose, and exhale slowly through your mouth.

- Focus on your breath. Pay attention to the sensation of the air moving in and out of your body. If your mind wanders, gently redirect your attention back to your breath.

- Try to let go of any thoughts or judgments that come up. Just notice them and let them pass, like clouds in the sky.

- Continue to focus on your breath for as long as you like. You can start with a few minutes and gradually work up to longer periods of time.

It's important to remember that meditation is a skill that takes practice. Don't worry if you find it difficult at first, or if your mind wanders. Just keep coming back to your breath. With time and practice, you will likely find that meditation helps to reduce anxiety and improve overall well-being.

# MENTAL GROUNDING: DAYDREAM

Daydreaming can be a helpful way to reduce anxiety in some situations, as it can allow you to take a break from the demands of the present moment and find some mental space to relax. However, it's important to keep in mind that excessive daydreaming can also be a sign of avoidance or escapism, and it's not a replacement for dealing with anxiety in a healthy and effective way.

Here is how you can use daydreaming as a way to reduce anxiety:

- ☑ Find a quiet, comfortable place to sit or lie down, where you won't be interrupted.
- ☑ Close your eyes and take several deep breaths to relax your body and mind.
- ☑ Let your thoughts wander and visualize a place or experience that brings you peace and happiness. This can be a real place you've visited before, or a place you've imagined in your mind.
- ☑ Spend a few minutes in this daydream, allowing yourself to fully immerse in the experience and let go of any worries or stress.
- ☑ When you're ready, slowly open your eyes and take a few more deep breaths.

It's important to remember that daydreaming should not be used as a way to avoid dealing with anxiety or other difficult emotions. If you find that you're relying on daydreaming as a way to escape from reality, it may be helpful to speak with a mental health professional.

# COUNTING

Counting can be a simple and effective way to reduce anxiety in the moment. Here's how you can use it:

- ✓ Close your eyes and take several deep breaths to relax your body and mind.
- ✓ As you exhale, silently count backwards from 10 to 1. Focus on the numbers and the act of counting, rather than any anxious thoughts or worries.
- ✓ When you reach 1, start the counting over again from 10. Continue this process for a few minutes, or longer if you wish.
- ✓ When you're ready, slowly open your eyes and take a few more deep breaths.

Counting can help to ground you in the present moment and provide a mental focus, which can help to distract you from anxious thoughts and emotions. It's a simple technique that you can use anytime and anywhere, and it can be especially helpful when you're feeling overwhelmed or anxious.

# ANXIETY FREE - MASTER YOUR FEELINGS

Emotion recognition is the process of identifying and understanding your emotions and how they affect your thoughts and behaviors. This can be a helpful tool for controlling anxiety because it can help you become more aware of your emotional states and learn how to manage them in a healthy way.

Here are a few steps you can take to use emotion recognition to control anxiety:

- ☑ Pay attention to your emotional states: Start by noticing how you feel throughout the day. Pay attention to your physical sensations, such as racing heart or shallow breathing, as well as your emotional experiences, such as worry or fear.

- ☑ Name your emotions: Practice labeling your emotions with specific words. This can help you better understand and differentiate between different emotional states.

- ☑ Reflect on the causes of your emotions: Consider what might have triggered your emotional state and what underlying needs or values may be driving your feelings.

- ☑ Practice managing your emotions: Once you have identified and named your emotions, try using specific strategies to manage them in a healthy way. This might involve using relaxation techniques, finding healthy ways to cope with stress, or seeking support from others.

- ☑ Reflect on your emotional patterns: As you practice emotion recognition and management, take some time to reflect on your emotional patterns. Are there certain triggers or situations that tend to cause you more anxiety? Are there any patterns in your coping strategies that might be helpful or unhelpful?

# JOURNALING

Journaling can be a helpful tool for managing anxiety because it allows you to process and express your thoughts and feelings in a safe, private place.

Here are some steps you can follow to use journaling to cope with anxiety:

 Set aside a specific time each day to write in your journal. Some people find it helpful to write first thing in the morning, while others prefer to write in the evening before bed. Choose a time that works best for you.

- ☑ Find a quiet, comfortable place to write. You may want to find a spot in your home where you can sit and write without being interrupted.

- ☑ Begin by writing down your anxiety-provoking thoughts and feelings. Don't worry about writing in complete sentences or using perfect grammar. Just write whatever comes to mind.

- ☑ Try to identify any patterns or themes that emerge as you write. For example, you may notice that your anxiety is often triggered by certain types of situations or events.

- ☑ Write about possible solutions or coping strategies for managing your anxiety. You might try brainstorming a list of different ways you could respond to anxiety-provoking situations.

Mood tracking is the process of regularly monitoring and recording your mood over time. This can be a helpful tool for understanding your emotional patterns and identifying potential triggers for negative mood states.

Here are some steps you can take to use mood tracking:

- ☑ Choose a mood tracking method: There are a variety of ways you can track your mood, such as using a mood journal or an app on your phone. Consider what method will be most convenient and effective for you.

- ☑ Set a regular time for tracking: Choose a specific time each day to track your mood. This might be first thing in the morning, at the end of the day, or at some other regular interval.

- ☑ Record your mood: Use your chosen tracking method to record your mood at the designated time. You can rate your mood on a scale (such as 1-10), write a few sentences about how you are feeling, or use a specific system for categorizing your mood (such as using symbols or colors).

- ☑ Record potential mood triggers: Along with tracking your mood, consider noting any potential triggers or events that might have influenced your mood. This might include things like sleep patterns, stressors, or interactions with others.

- ☑ Review your mood tracking: After tracking your mood for a period of time, review your records to look for patterns or trends. Do you notice any specific triggers for negative mood states? Are there any activities or habits that seem to be associated with improved mood?

By tracking your mood regularly, you can gain a better understanding of your emotional patterns and identify potential strategies for managing your mood in a healthy way.

# EMOTION DEFUSION

Emotional defusion is a technique used in acceptance and commitment therapy (ACT) to help you disentangle from negative thoughts and emotions. It involves observing your thoughts and emotions as separate from your sense of self, rather than getting caught up in or identifying with them.

Here are some steps you can take to practice emotional defusion:

- ☑ Notice your negative thoughts: Pay attention to the negative thoughts that arise in your mind, particularly those that are recurrent or distressing.

- ☑ Label your thoughts: Practice labeling your thoughts with phrases such as "I am having the thought that..." or "I am noticing the thought that..." This helps to create distance between you and the thought, and reminds you that you are not your thoughts.

- ☑ Imagine your thoughts as objects: Try visualizing your thoughts as objects that you can observe and let pass by, rather than getting caught up in them. You might imagine them as clouds in the sky or leaves floating down a stream.

# ANXIETY FREE - BEHAVIORAL TOOLS

## SMART GOALS

SMART goals are specific, measurable, achievable, relevant, and time-bound goals that can be used to help you plan and achieve your objectives. Using SMART goals as a planner can be a helpful tool for reducing anxiety because it can provide a sense of structure and direction, and help you break down larger goals into more manageable steps.

Here are some steps you can take to use SMART goals as a planner to reduce anxiety:

- ✓ Identify a specific goal that you want to work towards: This might be a goal related to reducing anxiety, such as "I want to learn how to manage my anxiety symptoms more effectively."

- ✓ Make the goal specific: Consider what specifically you want to achieve with your goal. For example, "I want to learn specific techniques for managing anxiety, such as deep breathing and progressive muscle relaxation."

- ✓ Make the goal measurable: Determine how you will measure your progress towards your goal. This might involve tracking your anxiety symptoms on a scale, keeping a journal of your anxiety-reducing techniques, or setting specific milestones for yourself.

- ☑ Make the goal achievable: Consider whether your goal is realistic and achievable given your current resources and constraints. If the goal feels too daunting or unrealistic, try breaking it down into smaller, more achievable steps.

- ☑ Make the goal relevant: Make sure that your goal aligns with your values and is something that you are motivated to work towards. This will help you stay committed and engaged with the goal.

- ☑ Make the goal time-bound: Set a specific deadline for achieving your goal. This will help you stay focused and motivated, and allow you to track your progress over time.

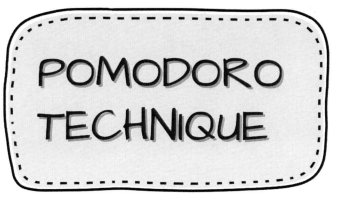

The Pomodoro Technique is a time management method that involves working in focused bursts of time followed by short breaks. This technique can be a helpful tool for reducing anxiety because it can help you stay organized and focused, and reduce the overwhelming feeling that can come with trying to tackle a large or complex task.

Here are some steps you can take to use the Pomodoro Technique as a planner to reduce anxiety:

- ☑ Identify a specific task that you want to work on: This might be a task related to reducing anxiety, such as researching anxiety management techniques or creating a plan for managing your anxiety symptoms.

- ☑ Set a timer for around 25 minutes: This is the length of a Pomodoro "sprint". During this time, focus solely on the task at hand, without any distractions.

- ☑ Take a short break: When the timer goes off, take a 5-10 minute break to rest and recharge. You might take this time to stretch, take a walk, or do something else to help you relax.

- ☑ Repeat the process: After your break, set the timer for another 25-minute sprint and continue working on your task. Repeat this process until you have completed 4 Pomodoros (sprints).

- ☑ Take a longer break: After completing 4 Pomodoros, take a longer break (20-30 minutes) to rest and recharge.

# EISENHOWER MATRIX

The Eisenhower Matrix is a method used to prioritize tasks based on their level of importance and urgency. It can be helpful for managing time and reducing stress because it helps you focus on the most important tasks and make better use of your time.

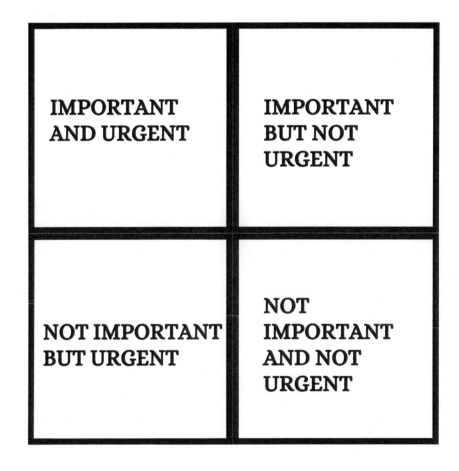

**Eisenhower Matrix:**

Draw a box with four quadrants.

In the top left quadrant, write "Important and Urgent." In the top right quadrant, write "Important but Not Urgent." In the bottom left quadrant, write "Not Important but Urgent." In the bottom right quadrant, write "Not Important and Not Urgent."

Write down all of the tasks that you need to complete in the next week or month.

Assign each task to one of the quadrants according to its level of importance and urgency. For example, tasks that are both important and urgent should go in the top left quadrant. Tasks that are not urgent but important should go in the top right quadrant.

Review the tasks in each quadrant and decide how you will handle them. For tasks in the top left quadrant (Important and Urgent), you should either do them right away or delegate them to someone else. Tasks in the top right quadrant (Important but Not Urgent) should be scheduled for later. Tasks in the bottom left quadrant (Not Important but Urgent) can be delegated to someone else or eliminated if possible. Tasks in the bottom right quadrant (Not Important and Not Urgent) should be eliminated.

By using the Eisenhower Matrix, you can focus on the most important tasks and minimize distractions, which can help you manage your time more effectively and reduce stress. It's important to review and update your matrix regularly to ensure that you are staying on track and focusing on the right tasks.

# TIME-BOXED WORRY

Setting aside dedicated "worry time" can be a helpful strategy for managing anxiety and avoiding the tendency to worry all the time. Here are some steps you can follow to set aside time for worry:

- Choose a specific time and place for your worry time. Some people find it helpful to schedule worry time at the same time each day, while others prefer to do it on an as-needed basis. You might choose a quiet room in your home or a secluded outdoor spot as your worry time location.

- During worry time, allow yourself to worry about anything and everything that's on your mind. Write down your worries in a journal or on a piece of paper. Don't censor your thoughts or try to talk yourself out of worrying. Just let the worries flow.

- Set a time limit for worry time. You might start with 15-20 minutes and adjust as needed. When your worry time is up, close your journal or put away your worry list and try to let go of your worries for the rest of the day.

- Practice mindfulness techniques to help you stay in the present moment and let go of your worries. This might include deep breathing, focusing on your senses, or repeating a mantra to yourself.

- When worries pop into your head outside of worry time, remind yourself that you have a designated time to worry later and try to let the worry go for now. You might also try redirecting your attention to something else, such as a task or activity.

- It may take some practice to get used to setting aside dedicated worry time, but over time it can help you feel more in control of your worries and reduce your overall anxiety.

# ANCHORING TOOLS: YOUR SYMBOL

Using a mark that you've drawn on your hand as an anchor, or a physical reminder to stay present and focused, can be a helpful strategy for reducing anxiety. Here are some steps you can follow to use this technique:

- Choose a mark that you can draw on the back of your hand with a pen or marker. It could be a simple dot, a line, or a symbol that has personal meaning to you.

- When you start to feel anxious, take several deep breaths and focus your attention on the mark on your hand. Try to observe it without judgment, as if you are seeing it for the first time.

- If your thoughts wander or your anxiety starts to increase, gently redirect your attention back to the mark on your hand.

- As you focus on the mark, try to allow your anxious thoughts and feelings to be there without getting caught up in them. Instead, focus on the present moment and the physical sensation of the mark on your hand.

- Using the mark on your hand as an anchor can help you stay present and focused, which can in turn help reduce anxiety. It may take some practice to get the hang of this technique, but over time it can become a helpful tool for managing anxiety in daily life.

Anchoring is a technique used in cognitive-behavioral therapy that involves focusing on a specific object, thought, or sensation in the present moment to help you stay grounded and reduce anxiety. Here's an example of how you might use anchoring to reduce anxiety:

- Let's say you are about to give a presentation at work and you are feeling anxious about it. As you start to feel anxious, you might try the following:

- Notice the physical sensations of anxiety in your body, such as a racing heart, shallow breathing, or tense muscles.

- Choose an anchor, such as a specific object in your surroundings or a mantra that you repeat to yourself. For example, you might focus on a plant on the windowsill or repeat the phrase "I am calm and in control" to yourself.

- Take several deep breaths and focus your attention on your anchor. As you do this, try to allow your anxious thoughts and feelings to be there without getting caught up in them.

- If your thoughts wander or your anxiety starts to increase again, gently redirect your attention back to your anchor.

- By focusing on an anchor in your surroundings and allowing yourself to experience anxiety without getting overwhelmed by it, you can help reduce your overall anxiety. It may take some practice to get the hang of anchoring, but over time it can become a helpful tool for managing anxiety in daily life.

# PAST SELF

Anchoring yourself to your past self involves using memories of past successes or coping strategies to help reduce anxiety in the present moment. Here are some steps you can follow to anchor yourself to your past self to reduce anxiety:

- Think back to a time in the past when you faced a similar situation or challenge and were able to cope with it effectively. It could be a time when you gave a successful presentation, faced a difficult exam, or navigated a stressful event.

- Take several deep breaths and try to vividly remember the details of that experience. What did you do to cope with the situation? How did you feel afterwards?

- Use your past self as a source of strength and inspiration in the present moment. Remind yourself that you have faced challenges before and have the skills and resilience to do so again.

- Use the coping strategies that you used in the past to help reduce your anxiety in the present. For example, if you used deep breathing or positive self-talk to cope with stress in the past, you might try using those strategies again.

- By anchoring yourself to your past self and using past successes and coping strategies as a guide, you can help reduce anxiety in the present moment and build confidence in your ability to cope with challenges.

Opposite action is a technique used in dialectical behavior therapy (DBT) to help you manage difficult emotions by taking action that is opposite to the emotion you are feeling. This technique can be helpful in dealing with emotional urges because it can help you regulate your emotions and reduce the intensity of your emotional responses. Here are some steps you can take to use opposite action to deal with emotional urges:

Identify the emotion you are feeling: Notice what emotion you are experiencing and try to label it with a specific word, such as anger, sadness, or fear.

Identify the action that the emotion is urging you to take: Notice what you feel like doing as a result of the emotion, such as lashing out, withdrawing, or avoiding something.

Consider the long-term consequences of taking the urged action: Reflect on the potential consequences of acting on the emotional urge. Will it help you achieve your goals or lead to negative outcomes?

Take the opposite action: Based on your reflection, choose an action that is opposite to the emotional urge. For example, if you are feeling angry and want to lash out, you might try calming yourself down with deep breathing or taking a break from the situation. If you are feeling anxious and want to avoid something, you might try facing the fear or anxiety head-on in a controlled way.

Reflect on the results: After taking the opposite action, reflect on the results. Did the action help you regulate your emotions and reduce the intensity of your emotional response?

# GRADED EXPOSURE

★★★★☆

Creating a list of activities or situations and rating them can be a helpful strategy for reducing anxiety because it allows you to identify and prioritize your worries and develop a plan for managing them. Here's how you can use this technique:

- Make a list of the activities or situations that are causing you anxiety. Be as specific as possible.

- Rate each item on your list according to how anxious it makes you feel, using a scale of 1-10 (1 being not anxious at all and 10 being extremely anxious).

- Look for patterns or themes on your list. Are there certain types of activities or situations that consistently cause you high levels of anxiety?

- For items on your list that are rated high in anxiety (8 or above), brainstorm potential solutions or coping strategies. These might include seeking the help of a mental health professional, developing relaxation techniques, or finding ways to modify the activity or situation to make it more manageable.

- For items on your list that are rated lower in anxiety (7 or below), consider whether you can eliminate them from your list or approach them with a more positive mindset.

By creating and rating a list of activities or situations, you can gain insight into what is causing your anxiety and develop a plan for managing it. This can help you feel more in control and reduce your overall anxiety.

Soothing yourself and talking kindly to yourself is a form of self-compassion, which is the practice of being understanding and caring towards yourself, especially during difficult times. Self-compassion can be helpful for reducing anxiety because it helps you feel supported and cared for, rather than criticized or judged.

Here are some ways you can practice self-compassion to reduce your anxiety:

- Treat yourself the way you would a good friend. If a friend was struggling with anxiety, you would likely offer them words of encouragement and support. Try to do the same for yourself.

- Practice self-kindness. Rather than berating yourself for feeling anxious or criticizing yourself for not being able to "fix" your anxiety, try to be understanding and compassionate towards yourself.

- Use self-soothing techniques. These might include taking deep breaths, finding a comfortable place to sit or lie down, or using a soothing touch, such as a hug or a warm blanket.

- Remind yourself that it's okay to feel anxious. It's a natural and common human emotion, and everyone experiences anxiety at some point.

- By practicing self-compassion, you can reduce your anxiety by feeling more supported and cared for, rather than harshly judged. It's important to remember that you deserve the same kindness and understanding that you would extend to a good friend.

By creating and rating a list of activities or situations, you can gain insight into what is causing your anxiety and develop a plan for managing it. This can help you feel more in control and reduce your overall anxiety.

# Help Others

Encourage the person to talk about their feelings and thoughts. Providing a safe and supportive environment where they can express themselves can be a great way to help them cope with anxiety.

Help the person identify and challenge negative thoughts. Many people with anxiety have distorted or irrational thinking patterns, and helping them identify and reframe these thoughts can be a useful strategy for managing their anxiety.

Encourage the person to engage in relaxation techniques, such as progressive muscle relaxation or deep breathing. These techniques can help reduce physical symptoms of anxiety, such as rapid heart rate or difficulty breathing.

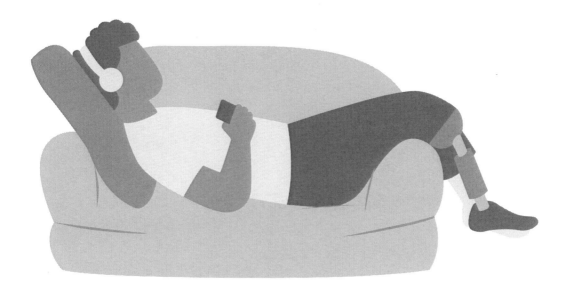

Help the person develop a plan for managing anxiety-provoking situations. This can include strategies such as identifying and avoiding triggers, developing coping statements, and practicing relaxation techniques in advance.

Encourage the person to engage in regular physical activity and to adopt healthy lifestyle habits, such as getting enough sleep, eating a healthy diet, and limiting caffeine and alcohol intake.

Encourage the person to seek professional help if their anxiety is severe or debilitating. A mental health professional, such as a therapist or counselor, can provide more specialized support and treatment for anxiety disorders.

# Quotes on Positive Thinking

"Happiness is not something ready made. It comes from your own actions." - Dalai Lama

"The only way to do great work is to love what you do." - Steve Jobs

"Be the change you wish to see in the world." - Mahatma Gandhi

"Believe you can and you're halfway there." - Theodore Roosevelt

"The power of positive thinking is undeniable. When you think positively, you automatically feel happier and more motivated." - Unknown

"An attitude of positive expectation is the mark of the superior personality." - Brian Tracy

"Positive thinking is not about expecting the best to happen every time, but accepting that whatever happens is the best for this moment." - Zig Ziglar

"Success is not the key to happiness. Happiness is the key to success." - Albert Schweitzer

# Quotes on Positive Thinking

""Your positive action combined with positive thinking results in success." - Shiv Khera

"The most powerful weapon on earth is the human soul on fire." - Ferdinand Foch

"A positive attitude may not solve all your problems, but it will annoy enough people to make it worth the effort." - Herm Albright

# Positive Affirmations

"I am worthy and deserving of love and happiness."

"I am capable and strong."

"I am in control of my thoughts and actions."

"I am confident and successful in all that I do."

"I am grateful for all the abundance in my life."

"I am surrounded by positivity and good energy."

"I am at peace with myself and those around me."

"I am constantly learning and growing."

"I am deserving of a healthy and fulfilling life."

"I am worthy of achieving my goals and dreams."

# Online Resources

**MENTAL HEALTH**

National Alliance on Mental Illness (NAMI) - www.nami.org

Mental Health America (MHA) - www.mentalhealthamerica.net

American Psychological Association (APA) - www.apa.org

Substance Abuse and Mental Health Services Administration (SAMHSA) - www.samhsa.gov

National Institute of Mental Health (NIMH) - www.nimh.nih.gov

World Health Organization (WHO) - www.who.int
Mind - www.mind.org.uk

Anxiety and Depression Association of America (ADAA) - www.adaa.org

# Online Resources

Center for Mental Health Services (CMHS) - www.samhsa.gov/cmhs

International Association for Suicide Prevention (IASP) - www.iasp.info

**ANXIETY**

Kids Health - www.kidshealth.org/en/teens/anxiety.html

Anxiety and Depression Association of America (ADAA) - www.adaa.org/living-with-anxiety/children

National Institute of Mental Health (NIMH) - www.nimh.nih.gov/health/topics/anxiety-disorders/index.shtml

Child Mind Institute - www.childmind.org/en/topics/anxiety

# Online Resources

Kids Help Phone - www.kidshelpphone.ca/topics/anxiety/

Teens Health - www.teenshealth.org/en/teens/anxiety-disorders.html

Young Minds - www.youngminds.org.uk/find-help/conditions/anxiety-in-young-people/

ReachOut - www.reachout.com/anxiety-and-depression

Mental Health Foundation - www.mentalhealth.org.uk/a-to-z/a/anxiety

Made in United States
North Haven, CT
30 June 2023

38417272R00059